SECOND NATURE
CHANGES & CHALLENGES IN THE NEW ENVIRONMENT

Clear
Choices
THE WATER YOU DRINK

By Matthew Higgins
with Mark Stewart

NORWOODHOUSE PRESS

All photos are courtesy of Getty, except for the following:
Photo Credits: Deposit Photos (16, 22, 32, 33); Black Book Partners archives (18); Joe Burull (35); Sidwell Friends School (36); Water.org (44).

Cover: Deposit Photos

Special thanks to Content Consultant Ashley McDowell.

Library of Congress Cataloging-in-Publication Data

Higgins, Matthew.
  Clear choices : the water you drink / by Matthew Higgins, Mark Stewart.
      p. cm. -- (Second nature)
  Includes bibliographical references and index.
  Summary: "In many countries, safe drinkable water is not a guarantee. This book looks at the challenges to the world water supply, and the far-reaching environmental, commercial and political costs if those challenges are not met. Among the topics covered are problems of population growth and climate change"--Provided by publisher.
  ISBN-13: 978-1-59953-450-3 (library edition : alk. paper)
  ISBN-10: 1-59953-450-9 (library edition : alk. paper)
1. Drinking water--Juvenile literature. 2. Water-supply--Juvenile literature. I. Stewart, Mark, 1960- II. Title.
  TD348.H49 2011
  363.6'1--dc23
                            2011017622

Manufactured in the United States of America in North Mankato, Minnesota.
176N—072011

COVER: Water may be our most precious resource. Every drop can be used in a way that helps people, animals, and plants.

Contents

Words in **bold type** are defined on page 46.

1 What's the Problem?

WATER SOURCES AT RISK

Living things need water to survive. Some need a little, and others need a lot. Even more important than the quantity of that water is the quality of it. The cleaner and clearer water is, the healthier it will be for plants, animals, and, of course, humans. In some parts of the world, access to clean water is as simple as turning the handle on a faucet. In other parts, people devote much of their energy to finding drinkable water on a daily basis.

Humans are fortunate because many of us have control over the quantity and quality of the water we use. Plants and animals do not enjoy this same "luxury." They use what the environment gives them. Over millions of years, different species have evolved in ways that help them thrive on the amount of water that is available. If human activity changes that amount—or pollutes the water—these species have to adapt to survive. In many cases, they simply cannot.

Millions of people around the world, including this boy in Africa, must walk miles just for a chance to access clean water.

For humans to survive, they need access to a dependable water supply. They also must make sure the plants and animals they depend on get enough water. People have understood this for thousands of years. And yet, many scientists are predicting that clean water will one day become the world's most precious **commodity**. Some believe it already is.

A COMBINATION OF TROUBLES

The greatest challenges to clean water include pollution, **climate change**, increasing population, and **water management**. All of these problems are related, which makes solving them even trickier. For example, China is the largest and fastest-growing country in the world. The government encourages factories to be as productive as possible. But the Chinese do not have tough rules when it comes to pollution control. In fact, more than 20 billion tons of industrial wastewater is pumped into the Yangtze River each year. The Yangtze is China's longest river, and large cities such as Shanghai depend on it for drinking water. The country has more than 1.3 billion people. They cannot survive without clean water.

Meanwhile, climate change may also be having a huge impact on the quantity and quality of China's water supply. For instance, research has shown that glaciers in Tibet are melting at an **accelerated** pace, yet they are not **regenerating** as quickly. These glaciers feed many of

The Yangtze River in China has been crippled by pollution. Many of the fish that swim in it are now on the endangered species list.

China's rivers. If the Chinese people cannot count on their traditional water sources to meet their needs, they face major problems.

The news about climate change is especially discouraging for people in rural parts of China. Populations are growing rapidly in these regions, while the supply of drinkable water is not. Because people who live in these areas are poor, they do not have many choices when it comes to water management. They are not likely to get the latest technology to improve their water. Where there is not enough clean water, you will almost always find hunger, disease, and poverty.

CLOSER TO HOME

Environmental scientists have noted that over the past 50 years, precipitation has increased an average of 5 percent in the United States. Does that mean everyone is getting a little more rain? *No*. Northern areas have been getting wetter, while southern and western areas have been getting drier.

Many scientists attribute this **disparity** to climate change. Weather patterns have become more extreme and unpredictable. Precipitation statistics reflect this development. As a result, climate change could have a significant effect on the U.S. water supply 50 years from now.

An unpredictable water supply leads to another problem facing cities and towns throughout the country—most water management systems are outdated. They were designed when the demand for water was not as great as it is today. As populations have increased and pollutants have multiplied, many of these systems no longer suit modern needs. For

A burst pipe outside of Washington, D.C., sends water cascading down a road. These kinds of failures can cause significant damage.

example, a huge amount of water escapes because of leaks, **evaporation**, and other causes. In some cases, it makes more sense to rebuild a system than try to address problems one at a time.

What's in a drop of water?

You can't always tell if water is safe to drink by looking at it. In most developed countries, however, there is little need to worry. The water supplied to homes and businesses is safe to drink—though only a small percentage is actually used for drinking.

In developing countries, water must be boiled or purified before it is used for drinking or preparing food. But not everyone understands the importance of taking these steps. Nearly two million people a year die from diseases that come from contaminated water. Just as alarming, more than a billion people do not have access to safe drinking water.

In most modern countries, water goes through a treatment process before it comes out of a tap. This eliminates harmful **bacteria** that live in many water supplies. It also filters out polluting chemicals. These can build up in the body and also make the water taste bad.

Christchurch, New Zealand, used to be among the few cities in the world that had water clean enough to drink "raw." Its water comes from nearby mountains and is filtered naturally as it seeps into the ground. But all water sources are precious. When an earthquake struck Christchurch in 2011, its water supply was damaged severely. It will be many years before the city fully recovers.

A Christchurch resident gets water from a pump on his property. Finding clean water has become a problem for many people in this New Zealand town.

DROUGHT

Sometimes the climate can change very quickly in a region—and with little warning. When the amount of rainfall drops sharply in an area for a period of months or years, it is called a drought. The people, plants, and animals in a drought-stricken region find themselves fighting for their lives.

In some places, lakes and rivers disappear and wells run dry. Without rainwater for their fields, farmers must bring water in from somewhere else, usually by truck or train. This is extremely expensive and sometimes impossible. Crops often just die. It's not hard to see why a drought can trigger a crisis.

Droughts can happen almost anywhere. In the 1930s, a drought in the central United States was so bad that soil on farms dried up and blew away. For the past few decades, much of the Southwest in the United States has been affected by drought conditions.

Because of drought and rising demand from nearby cities, the water in Lake Mead in Nevada has dropped to its lowest level since the 1930s.

WORLD VIEW

In developed countries such as the United States, it is usually easy to get a glass of clean water. But there are many places on the planet where this is not the case. In fact, more than 1 billion people worldwide do not have access to safe drinking water. Regions of Asia and Africa have been hit hardest by this problem.

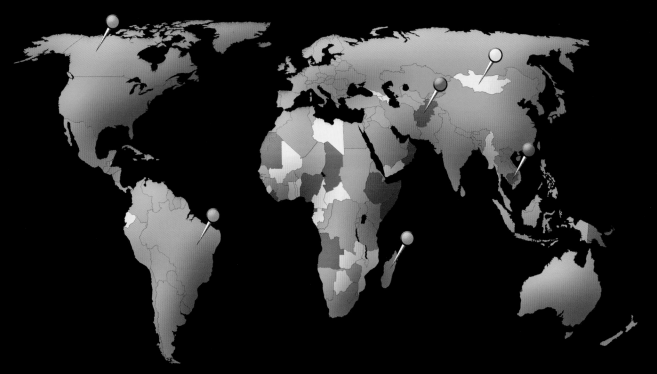

Percentage of Population with Access to Safe Drinking Water

Over 90% with safe water	45%–59% with safe water
75%–89% with safe water	30%–44% with safe water
60%–74% with safe water	Under 30% with safe water

Percentage of Population with Access to Safe Drinking Water

Canada
100%

Brazil
85%

Mongolia
62%

Madagascar
50%

Cambodia
41%

Afghanistan
13%

0%   25%   50%   75%   100%

NOTE: Data compiled by the Pacific Institute

WORLD VIEW

2 How We Got Here
THE STRUGGLE TO KEEP WATER SAFE

People have always lived as close as possible to reliable sources of fresh water. In early human history, this meant building settlements on or near rivers, lakes, and streams. With the start of farming, it became crucial for humans to learn how to transport clean water from these sources to their fields and also to homes located far away.

The first great cities were built in the Middle East, in an area called the Fertile Crescent (below). These lands were fed by three rivers: the Tigris, the Euphrates, and the Jordan. The water flow started in the mountains to the north. Reservoirs, canals, and **irrigation** ditches provided enough water for many thousands of people living together in the same community. The same technology later helped the great cities of ancient Egypt grow along the Nile River.

FERTILE CRESCENT

Mediterranean Sea

Egypt

Saudi Arabia

The Tigris River has been one of the primary sources of clean, fresh water in the Middle East since ancient times.

The Romans built their aqueducts to last. The Pont du Gard
is still standing in France.

WATER WAYS

In Roman times (about 2,000 years ago), engineers built
thousands of stone bridges to connect land over water.
These same builders constructed stone bridges to carry
clean water over land from mountain streams to far-away

cities. These structures were called aqueducts. We still use this word to describe systems designed to carry water over long distances. Aqueducts must be built to last—people depend on them for all their water needs. That was not a problem in Rome. Many of their aqueducts outlasted the Roman Empire. Some are still around today, including the Pont du Gard in France.

Stone aqueducts brought water to Roman homes, where it traveled through pipes made of lead, a soft metal that was easy to bend and shape. But there was a problem with lead—it's a toxic metal, and drinking water containing high amounts of lead is dangerous. Amazingly, there is evidence that the Romans knew about the dangers posed by this kind of pollution. Before water entered a home, it emptied into

Point and Non-Point

In the United States, the dangers of water pollution were recognized in the 1880s. However, it was not until the 1940s that the first federal laws were passed to punish polluters—and not until the 1970s and 1980s that these laws had much effect. The government focused on curbing water pollution from "point sources," such as waste treatment plants and factories.

Pollution from "non-point sources" is still a major problem. Non-point sources include water from heavy rains and water that runs off from farms and golf courses. In each of these cases, chemicals that were never meant to be consumed by humans end up entering our drinking-water supply.

Cholera has been a risk for centuries. This illustration from the 1800s shows a victim of the disease being helped into an ambulance.

a catch basin. This allowed impurities to sink slowly to the bottom. Romans may have also understood that exposing their water to air on its long journey helped purify it.

DANGERS OF DIRTY WATER

The Romans knew what almost every culture before and after did—that the greatest danger to human drinking water comes from humans themselves. When someone uses a source of drinking water in an unsafe way, it can put everyone in the community at risk. For example, the bacteria and pathogens from human waste can be deadly. Scientists were able to confirm this fact after the microscope was invented at the end of the 1600s. For the first time, humans could see how many microorganisms were swimming around in a drop of water.

Still, understanding the problem of polluted water and treating it were two different issues. In 1854, 616 people died during a cholera **epidemic** in London, England. Cholera was not a new disease, but doctors mistakenly believed it was spread through unclean air. They already knew that people who lived near polluted water (which smelled bad) were more likely to suffer from the disease.

During the 1854 outbreak, a scientist named John Snow observed that the closer people lived to a water pump on Broad Street in London, the more likely they were to be infected. But water from that pump did not smell or taste bad. When city officials investigated, they found that the well beneath the pump had been dug a few feet from a **cesspit**, which was overflowing with human waste. This contaminated water—not air—was responsible for spreading the disease.

Cholera wasn't the only water-pollution problem people faced during the 1800s. During the Industrial Revolution, many factories were powered by rivers. Any waste products, including chemical waste and human waste, were dumped into the water. When these pollutants flowed downstream, the people who drank the water got sick. Over time, people moved in great numbers to the cities where the large factories were located. With so many businesses and people crammed into a small area, some water supplies became badly contaminated.

These conditions convinced most cities to build modern sewer systems, which treated wastewater before it was released back into the environment. This process prevented outbreaks of disease. However, it did not do much to keep dangerous chemicals out of the water. One of the problems with toxic chemicals is they build up in the body over time. It can take years before people show the effects of this condition and become seriously ill. Toxic chemicals also damage **ecosystems** by contaminating the food chain. When people eat fish from polluted waters, for example, the body absorbs the chemicals in the fish.

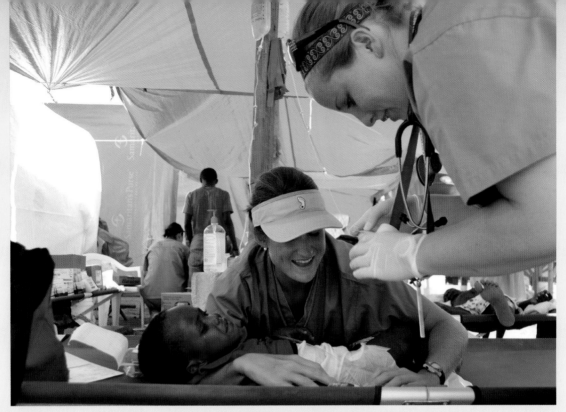

Medical workers in Haiti are glad they reached this young cholera victim before it was too late.

Earthquakes & Cholera

Knowing what makes drinking water dangerous does not always prevent people from getting sick. In 2010, a powerful earthquake shook the island nation of Haiti. Much of Haiti's water and **sanitation** systems were destroyed. About nine months after the earthquake, Haitian people began dying from cholera. No cases of the disease had been reported in the country for more than a generation. It spread because people were drinking water that was contaminated. In the ravaged country, many felt they didn't have a choice.

Cholera is serious business. If an outbreak becomes an epidemic, there often are not enough doctors or enough medicine to keep the disease under control. Cholera epidemics kill thousands of people worldwide every year.

3 If We Do Nothing

THE CONSEQUENCES OF DIRTY WATER

People who live in places where cool, clear water comes out of a fountain or faucet have a hard time appreciating what it's like to worry about having water to drink every day. They think of it as someone else's problem. Where water is concerned, however, "someone else's problem" has a way of becoming *your* problem in a hurry.

To ensure we have enough water in the future, we need to do a better job of keeping it safe and clean—not just for humans, but for all living things. We must also find ways to make safe, clean water available to more people. If we are unable to meet these challenges, the consequences could be disastrous.

THE POLLUTION PROBLEM

In most developed countries, there are laws that prevent the release of toxic chemicals directly into the water supply. Businesses may break these laws—and accidents occur—but the penalties are harsh, especially in the United States. Anyone who remembers polluted rivers, lakes, and streams in the 1950s and 1960s will tell you how much better things are today. Wildlife has rebounded

Rivers across the United States used to look like this one. Fortunately, we've realized that polluted water is one of our greatest environmental challenges.

Women look for usable items in India's Dal Lake. It used to be a tourist attraction, but pollution has turned it into a mess of muck and waste.

in areas where it was once endangered, and ecosystems in many areas that were once polluted have recovered.

Unfortunately, this is not the case in most developing countries. In India, for example, fewer than one in ten towns has any kind of sewage system. That means waste of all kinds empties into open water—the same water used for cooking, bathing, and drinking. Companies all over the world are moving businesses to India because its people are hard workers and well educated. It's also less expensive to do business there. But if the country does not improve how its **infrastructure** delivers safe water, those companies may move away. Jobs will disappear, and the standard of living will fall.

In China, another country where the government pushes for rapid business growth, chemical pollution is literally killing the rivers—and the people who drink from them. New factories seem to spring up every day. Many dump chemical waste directly into the environment instead of spending the money to dispose of it safely.

The Chinese government has made safe water a priority in recent years, but it continues to fall behind. One study showed that two million people had become sick from drinking water that contained high levels of arsenic, a chemical that causes skin cancer, lung cancer, and heart disease. Arsenic is used in a number of industries, including the manufacture of batteries and **pesticides**.

UP IN THE AIR

While chemical and human waste pose a threat to local water supplies, another type of pollution can also have an impact. The **emissions** from factory smokestacks and the tailpipes of cars and trucks contain chemical pollutants and **greenhouse gases**. As these emissions collect in the atmosphere, some of the

WHOSE JOB IS IT?

Whose responsibility is it to clean up the water supply in fast-growing nations like India and China? Some say that this job belongs to the government. It takes in money from companies that build factories, and it also collects money from working people in the form of taxes. Many believe governments should spend whatever it takes to safeguard the water supply.

Others argue that businesses should pay the bill. After all, they are getting the greatest benefit from the workers they hire. Why not spend some of those profits making sure workers are as healthy as possible? Still others say that solutions begin with the people. They need to stand up for their right to clean water. They must also understand how things they do may contaminate the water they depend on.

In the end, the answer is that improving the water supply is a partnership. People, businesses, and the government must work together and do what they can to find solutions.

Scientists are worried about how quickly the glaciers in the Himalaya Mountains are melting.

airborne chemicals fall back to earth in the form of acid rain. In many ecosystems, acid rain can change the **pH balance** of water, making it more acidic. This problem puts great stress on the plants and animals that live there.

When acid rain was first detected in the 1970s, it was not seen as an environmental problem. Since people drink soda with high levels of acid, no one thought much about dangers posed to the water supply. But studies showed that there was great cause for concern. For example, water with a high acid content dissolves the copper and lead contained in the pipes of homes, schools, and businesses. This can lead to unsafe water.

The more worrisome threat posed by greenhouse gases is to the overall climate. Environmental scientists disagree on how much the climate has changed as a result of greenhouse gases— or how rapidly it may change in the future. What everyone does agree on is that the climate changes we are witnessing now are affecting the world water supply, dropping it to very low levels in some areas.

One region of great concern is the Himalaya Mountains and the Tibetan Plateau, both in Asia. Glacier ice covers more than 40,000 square miles of this area, which is the source of fresh water for almost half the world's population. Each spring, the melting ice feeds many of the great rivers of Asia, including the Ganges, the Brahmaputra, the Indus, and the Mekong. Each winter, the glaciers "rebuild" with the heavy snows that blanket the region. At least, that's the way it used to work.

A recent survey of the Himalayas showed that almost 20 percent of the glaciers had disappeared in a 50-year period. Chinese scientists estimate that glaciers will decrease in the region by more than 40 percent by the year 2070. They think that warming temperatures in the high altitudes may be responsible for the shrinking glaciers. One thing is certain— less glacier ice each winter means less water each spring.

WATER... THE NEW OIL?

In your lifetime, it is very likely that you will see a shift of power in the world. Right now, countries that control the flow of oil have immense wealth and power. As more people turn to alternative energy, the influence these countries have in world affairs will be smaller. Who will "replace" them? Some say it will be countries rich in another natural resource: water.

Right now, almost 15 percent of the world's water is controlled by Brazil. Two other countries in South America, Colombia and Peru, are also rich in water. In North America, Canada may turn out to be a world water power. It has as much water as the United States but far fewer people who need it.

Cities such as Sitka, Alaska, may also be transformed as water becomes more precious. Sitka's Blue Lake holds trillions of gallons of crystal-clear water. With a population of 10,000, it will never use more than a tiny fraction of that water. Sitka has already begun shipping water to Mumbai, India. There the water is bottled and sold to drought-stricken regions of the Middle East.

4 Bright Ideas
HOW WE'RE MEETING OUR WATER NEEDS

A lot of smart, creative people are working on the problem of getting clean water to populations that need it. In some cases, those populations are in dry, remote areas. In others, there is water in abundance, but too many people are using it. Right now most of the solutions to the world's water problems involve improving existing infrastructure. But there are many exciting projects being developed for future water needs.

SOLVING PROBLEMS

The city of Phnom Penh in Cambodia solved its water problem by fixing what it already had. The city's water system, which serves one million people, had not been updated in 50 years. Much of it dated back to the 1890s. During several decades of war and political unrest, the system began to fall apart. More than 70 percent of the water in Phnom Penh's system never made it to the people because of leaky pipes and pumps. A 10-year project to

Residents of Phnom Penh celebrate during their annual Water Festival. The Cambodian city worked hard to fix problems with its water system.

WATER FROM AIR

Every day on our planet, billions of gallons of water evaporate into the air. It returns to earth in the form of precipitation. In some places, the air is so thick with water molecules you can feel it. In recent years, scientists and engineers have been working together to build machines that can "harvest" water from the atmosphere. These water generators rely on a process that is similar to the way rain is made.

Machines that generate water are used in places where fresh water is hard to find, or where fresh water is needed after disasters or emergencies. Right now it takes a lot of energy to run the condensers that pull the water from the air. However, people are working on designs that can use solar energy to power the entire process. This is important, because in places where people are desperate for water, electricity is often unavailable.

fix the system was a big success. Today, only about six percent of the city's water goes to waste.

In Singapore, people are drinking tap water that they had once flushed down the toilet. More than five million people live and work in this city-state in southeast Asia. With a large and growing population, the government worried that it would not have enough fresh water. So its Public **Utilities** Board asked scientists and engineers to work together to create a system that would enable residents to reuse water again and again.

The solution was a system that takes sewage water and purifies it with microfiltration, reverse osmosis, and ultraviolet disinfection. Microfiltration removes particles and impurities as waste water passes through tiny openings. Reverse osmosis is a process that separates water molecules from other

An employee of the Changi Water Reclamation Plant in Singapore shows off water before and after it has been cleansed.

molecules. It is often used to take the salt out of seawater. After microfiltration and reverse osmosis, an ultraviolet light is used to destroy any remaining bacteria. The wavelength of ultraviolet light is especially good at killing germs.

Not all waterborne bacteria are bad for you. In some cases, these one-celled organisms eat contaminants and help clean the water in a process called **bioremediation**. Liquid waste from factories containing oil and metals is filtered through membranes. During this process known as nanofiltration, hungry bacteria prevent the tiny holes from getting clogged. This keeps the membranes from having to be removed and cleaned.

SALT OUT OF WATER

Besides searching for the best methods for keeping water clean, scientists are exploring ways of making sure humans, plants, and animals will never run out of water. The obvious place to look is the earth's oceans. The problem is that ocean water contains large amounts of salt (or saline). Humans can't drink seawater because the body must use more water to flush out the salt than it takes in.

People have been taking the salt out of seawater for centuries. This process is called desalination. The trick is to do so on a large enough scale to provide drinkable water for large numbers of people. The most common form of desalination is distillation. In this process, seawater is heated until it evaporates. The vapors rise until they come in contact with a cool surface. The vapor

Large filters like these are used in the desalination process.

turns back into a liquid, but almost all of the salt is left behind after evaporation.

Right now there are desalination plants in more than 100 countries, including the United States. But they account for less than one percent of the world's fresh water. It takes a lot of energy to run a desalination plant. To produce enough water to quench the planet's thirst would require huge amounts of electricity.

For a time, scientists believed that nuclear power could be used. Today, they are looking at creating a new generation of desalination plants that would use renewable energy, including solar power. Other designs would be built around wind energy. Huge windmills would power reverse osmosis. Early experiments with this technology in the Netherlands have shown that one windmill can provide fresh water for 500 people a day.

Going Blue

A lot of water goes into the clothes you wear—both before and after you buy them. A pair of stonewashed jeans (below), for example, uses about 900 gallons during its lifetime. This includes the water used to grow the cotton, the water used to soften the jeans for sale, and the water used to clean them in your home.

In 2011, Levi Strauss & Co. substituted a gas called ozone for water to wash their jeans. They sell the jeans for the same price, but use 27% less water during this process. Multiply that by the millions of pairs the company expects to sell, and it's more than a drop in the bucket!

5 Trailblazers

These people are doing things to help keep our water clean today…and make the world better for tomorrow.

Ted Kuepper

Environmental Engineer

Kuepper runs a **humanitarian** organization called Global Water that makes safe water accessible to the poorest of the poor. His work focuses on bringing clean-water technologies to villages with no electricity. He oversees projects in developing countries all over the world.

Moshe Herzberg & Mohammed Saleem Ali-Shtayeh

Scientists

Herzberg is a professor at a university in Israel. Ali-Shtayeh is a professor in a Palestinian research center. The areas where they live are continually in conflict, but they see the value of cooperation. These two scientists discovered a process to make more clean water for everyone using less energy.

Sally Dominguez stands next to her invention, the Rainwater HOG.

Sally Dominguez

Inventor

Water is a precious resource, and space is too. Dominguez designed a storage device called the Rainwater HOG to make the most of both. It collects and stores rainwater from the roof of a house to be used for a variety of jobs.

Alexandre Allard & Danny Luong

Students

Allard and Luong are teenage students from Canada. They invented a way to use three kinds of bacteria together to break down **polystyrene** cups and containers that make their way into waterways. They were awarded the 2010 Stockholm Junior Water Prize for their discovery.

A lot of schools across the country have "gone green" in recent years. In other words, they have found ways to operate that are friendly to the environment. The very first was the Sidwell Friends School in Washington, D.C. In 2007, Sidwell's Middle School received a "platinum" rating from the U.S. Green Building Council. Engineers for the school worked with environmental scientists to create a wetland environment and then connected it with the school's water system.

The plants in this system do exactly what they do in a natural wetland—filter waste water. After working its way through this mini ecosystem, the water is clean enough to drink—although local laws don't allow it. Sidwell's science teachers are using the wetlands as an outdoor classroom. Meanwhile, the school has added solar panels, double-glazed windows, and other green features.

Since Sidwell went green, thousands of schools around the country have done the same, in many imaginative ways. Some states have created laws that say new school buildings must be environmentally friendly and energy efficient. Other states have made money available for schools to go green.

This wetland environment created by Sidwell's Middle School was part of a push to go green.

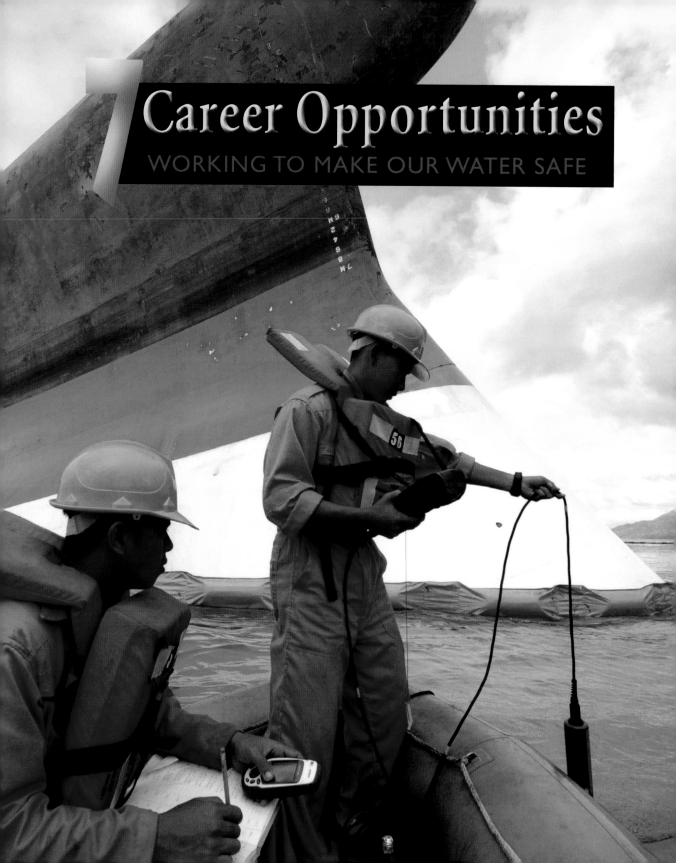

Career Opportunities

WORKING TO MAKE OUR WATER SAFE

When it comes to careers in water, there is good news and bad news. The good news is that there will be a huge number of jobs for skilled workers in this field in the years to come. The bad news is that we may never be able to fill all of these jobs. That's because the problems and challenges of getting clean water to the people who need it are likely to get worse before they get better.

CHEMISTRY & ENGINEERING

Keeping water safe is a job that often falls to chemists and engineers. Chemists must constantly monitor the water supply. Even the smallest changes can be a sign that something is wrong. Chemists can work in labs where hundreds of samples are tested every day. Or they can go out in the field as inspectors. Chemists also work for companies to make sure that they are not in violation of pollution laws.

A scientist takes a water sample during an investigation of a ferry accident off the coast of the Phillippines.

A New Partner

No matter what your special talent or interest, you can make a career out of making safe water available to the people who need it. Your partner in this job will be the United Nations. In 2010, the U.N. General Assembly announced that "safe and clean drinking water and sanitation is a human right essential to the full enjoyment of life and all other human rights." The U.N. called on its members to offer money, technology, and other resources to provide clean, accessible, and affordable drinking water and sanitation for everyone.

Engineers are responsible for designing and building the systems that keep toxic substances from entering the water supply. They also look at the best ways to build and repair water-delivery systems.

TREATING THE WATER

Often, the first sign that something is not right with the water supply is a change in the surrounding ecosystem. Detecting this type of change is a job for biologists and environmental scientists. They help companies and governments understand the impact of pollution on wildlife—and how water pollution can affect humans living nearby.

One of the most important jobs in the future will be building and operating water treatment plants. They take water from sewer pipes and then destroy microorganisms, chemical compounds, and other harmful materials. The people who operate these plants must understand how to read meters and gauges, know when to adjust chemicals

A worker inspects the water purification system
at a facility in Utah.

in the water (such as chlorine), take samples, and analyze
the water at different stages. They also have to know how
to fix equipment and what to do during emergencies.

8 Expert Opinions

When the best minds talk about the world's water supply, it's worth listening to what they say...

"Water is not only a basic necessity, it is a human right. Without water, there is no life. Yet hundreds of millions of people do not have access to safe, clean water."
—Ban Ki-moon, United Nations Secretary General, on the problem of getting clean water to people who need it

"Turn on the tap almost anywhere in America, and you'll get clean, safe water—a minor miracle on much of the planet."
—Bryan Walsh, journalist, on the ability to produce clean water in the United States

"We are in the process of developing a generation of kids who are environmental actors."
—Rose Ellis, Massachusetts educator, on how kids are being taught about our water needs

"It took a different kind of thinking, but the results are kind of amazing."
—*Carl Chiara, Levi Strauss executive, on his company's efforts to use less water*

"Many people thought there would be adequate time to adapt to less water. The lesson from Australia is that the shift has been very dramatic and has occurred in a very short period."
—*Ross Young, Executive Director of the Water Services Association of Australia, on decreasing water supplies in his country*

"More than 300 million rural residents throughout China still lack clean drinking water. In some areas, many farmers have to go several kilometers away to fetch drinking water, while some have to drink water with high fluorine or arsenic content or salty water that endangers their health."
—*Zhai Haohui, Chinese Government Minister, on how his country suddenly found itself in a water crisis*

LEFT: Ban Ki-moon   **ABOVE**: Carl Chiara

9 What Can I Do?

You don't have to be a scientist or an engineer to protect your local water supply. For example, you can remind adults to dispose of harmful waste products such as motor oil and old batteries in an environmentally friendly way. You can also encourage them to use outdoor products that are free of dangerous chemicals. Another thing that everyone can do is conserve water. For example, turn off the faucet when brushing your teeth. Water your lawn early in the morning or after sundown, when evaporation is slower.

If you would like to make a difference in the lives of people who do not have access to fresh water, there are ways to do that, too. Water.org is among the many charities bringing clean water to remote villages. This organization has projects in Africa, Asia, and the Caribbean. Many young people around the world work with this charity.

Water.org isn't the only organization that has created projects to improve the water supply in remote areas. National Geographic's Global Action Access is a good place to find these types of efforts. There are lots of ways to get involved, including starting a fundraising drive with classmates as a school project.

Matt Damon works with Water.org to help people who struggle everyday to get the water they need, including these children from Ethiopa.

Glossary

Accelerated—Sped up.

Bacteria—Single-celled microorganisms that live in soil, water, or bodies of plants and animals.

Bioremediation—The use of microorganisms to remove pollutants.

Cesspit—An area designated for sewage disposal.

Climate Change—A long-term change in weather conditions.

Commodity—Something useful or valued.

Disparity—Difference in quality or quantity.

Ecosystems—All the organisms, plants, and animals that make up specific ecological areas.

Emissions—Substances discharged into the air.

Epidemic—An outbreak of disease that affects many people and spreads quickly.

Evaporation—The process of expelling water and turning into vapor.

Greenhouse Gases—Gases that trap heat in the atmosphere, just as a greenhouse does during the winter.

Humanitarian—Affecting the health and well-being of people.

Infrastructure—The systems that work together to help a city or town run.

Irrigation—Systems designed for watering crops.

Pesticides—Chemicals used to kill bugs that feed on crops.

pH Balance—The measure of acid in a substance.

Polystyrene—A type of plastic.

Regenerating—Forming or creating again.

Sanitation—The maintenance of clean living conditions.

Utilities—Public services such as the delivery of electricity or water.

Water Management—The ways that a town, city, or country uses water.

Sources

The authors relied on many different books, magazines, and organizations to do research for this book. Listed below are the primary sources of information and their websites:

Anchorage Daily News	www.adn.com
BBC Asia-Pacific	news.bbc.co.uk/2/hi/asia-pacific
China Daily	www.chinadaily.com
National Geographic Magazine	www.nationalgeographic.com
Nature	www.nature.com
The New York Times	www.nytimes.com
Newsweek Magazine	www.newsweek.com
Science Magazine	www.sciencemag.org
Time Magazine	www.time.com
WaterHistory.org	www.waterhistory.org

Resources

To get involved with efforts to help the environment, you can contact these organizations:

Environmental Protection Agency	water.epa.gov
NASA Earth Observatory	earthobservatory.nasa.gov
UNICEF	www.unicef.org/wash
U.S. Geological Survey	water.usgs.gov
Water.org	www.water.org
The Water Project	www.thewaterproject.org

For more information on the subjects covered in this book:

Cartlidge, Cherese. *Water from Air: Water Harvesting Machines*. Chicago, Illinois. Norwood House Press, 2009.

Fradin, Judy & Dennis. *Witness to Disaster: Droughts*. Des Moines, Iowa. National Geographic Children's Books, 2008.

Gates, Alexander. *Encyclopedia of Pollution: Air, Earth, and Water*. New York, New York. Facts on File, 2011.

La Bella, Laura. *Not Enough to Drink: Pollution, Drought, and Tainted Water Supplies*. New York, New York. Rosen Publishing Group, 2007.

Index

Page numbers in **bold** refer to illustrations.

The Authors

DR. MATTHEW HIGGINS is an atmospheric scientist at the University of Colorado at Boulder. He specializes in Arctic climatology. Matt's doctorate is also from CU-Boulder, and he holds an undergraduate degree in chemical engineering from the University of Virginia. To help the environment, Matt often rides his bike to work.

MARK STEWART has written more than 200 non-fiction books for the school and library market. He has an undergraduate degree in History from Duke University. Mark's work in environmental studies includes books on the plants and animals of New York (where he grew up) and New Jersey (where he lives now).